Shouting At The Sea

Volume 3

Crime's
Against Poetry

Pablo Doherty

DEDICATION

For Mary Kate,
Terezita, Brogan, Ellen, Lorcan
and Donnacha

CONTENTS

To Be Like Only Him

Take a seasonal sabbatical
In the shadow of Mount Errigal
Whisper secret love amidst the Poison Glen
It's sensationally vocational
And extremely inspirational
To walk within the steps of fallen men

Watch early morning Glenveagh mist
Reclaim the earth that darkness kissed
To path the way and welcome home lost Gaels
Through trees of pine the spirits twist
And drum a beat with bloodied fist
To homage those who died neath Cahir's sails

We jump like salmon from the pier
In figure hugging rubber gear
And to the house we flee the biting midge
As daylight starts to disappear
We pack our magnet souvenir
To stick upon our ice dispensing fridge

Let dampened turf hang in the air
And leave its scent on cloth and hair
For in his eyes, this history starts to dim
His face can but reflect despair
That we in search of truth are there
To be like only him

Two Hits No Return

Memories came hurtling back
On the Lisburn road today
As Lorcan, he's my youngest son
Did turn around and say
A phase of such historic bent
Up there with the "Chinese burn"
As he stuck his brother on the thigh
"Two hits, no return"

What sparked this usually pleasant child
To act in such a way
Could it have been an accident
Or just boyish horseplay
Had Brogan, that's my eldest boy
Pushed a bit too far
"No that's not it" the lad replied
"I saw a yellow car"

Then with razor sharp precision
My daughter, full of charm
Gave two quick jabs without a blink
Upon her siblings arm
"No returns" my angel laughed
As we passed the Chelsea bar
While gesturing her finger
At a parked up yellow car

The little games we use to play
Have stood the test of time
I'm guessing other people's kids
Are just the same as mine
They're prone to disagreements
The odd argument and fight
But they always wish each other love
When they go to bed at night

Oi Citizen Of Blighty

Oi citizen of Blighty
Shift your arse out of that bed
Get picking fruit and vegetables
Amber Rudd has said
She wants a list of foreigners
So she can name and shame
Those folk taking up British jobs
And forcing you to claim

Attractive opportunities
For all the rank and file
So dust down those old overalls
And switch off Jeremy Kyle
Twenty four hour shift work
Is tailor made for you
Those crappy jobs that British snobs
Just wouldn't want to do

Walking home in the morning sun
Then sleep throughout the day
Never get to see your kids
And third world rates of pay
Packing food in the dead of night
Will get you off the bru
Build your skills and self respect
Instil some pride in you

So what about those immigrants
Who do the job today
She'll stick your body in their place
And send them on their way

Then All At Once The Beauty Of The World
It Did Reveal

Then all at once the beauty of the world it did reveal
On public transport, with the threat of heavy rain
They sat in silence staring at each other
Knowing life would never feel the same

"Look closely, even after several days of soap it still remains"
His name she wrote in biro on her wrist
She laughs and kicks her leg behind her heel
Then sneaks the fading ink a parting kiss

Break-time rendezvous in crowded halls
Leaning against lukewarm radiators
Our backs massaged by size four mitre balls
A flick of her hair turns us into fumbling fools
Engaged in a top of the table clash
Where we haven't learned the rules

Our friends refer to her with the prefix "your"
I've dreamed our life together in a premonition
And I no longer challenge their assumption
Accepting wilfully their affirmation
That I am now a couple,
And single is no more my definition

My tortuous need to slip her name
In each and every situation
Advising strangers of hourly whereabouts
Disregarding attempts to change direction of the conversation
Without hesitation I become an irritation

I am not affected by your opinion, only hers
As she avoids the easy path home
I take detours, for hours
Oblivious to the incessant showers
I welcome as my punishment the spray from passing cars
For someone else is sitting on the bus
And she is smiling, holding flowers

Jimmy's Homing Rat

I've a tale to tell, from some years back
In Bootle, it was at
Of two young lads from the Emerald Isle
And a foot long homing rat
Haughey's horse was an also ran
Limbo's money was all spent
They'd a few quid left for a carry out
And planned to skip the rent

Then they heard a call from down the hall
Of a damsel in distress
Who pulled the drawer for a pair of kaks
And found a wee brown mess
Well our heroes took the mantle up
With this squatter they would deal
And maybe get a cuddle
Some vino and a meal

Jimmy moved the furniture
And searched beneath her bed
Peter stood and scanned the room
With a saucepan on his head
Any sudden movements
Were met with sequels and screams
As Limbo told of rabid beasts
He'd seen on TV screens

With their manhood rightly questioned
As they danced around the floor
Hawkeye spied the furry fiend
Behind a cupboard door
The beast was cornered by some books
And a half chewed A4 folder
When it bared its teeth and took a leap
Right over Limbo's shoulder

Shams, save yourselves" the Braid man cried
As mayhem did ensue
The damsel headed for the pub
Followed by our two
Fuelled by several pints of stout
And the promise of some stew
Back to the house the lads did go
For they knew what they had to do

Peter, known for his brains
Jimmy, cunning as a fox
Somehow trapped their vermin guest
Inside an old shoe box
And as the sunrise slowly crept
To the tuneful Mersey beat
They took their game to the local train
And released it in the street

But they stood in sheer bewilderment
For they couldn't take much more
As the homing rat ran up the road
And back through their front door

There's A Killer Clown In Portstewart Town

There's a killer clown in Portstewart town
I met him last Friday night
Up by the Diamond at two am
And he gave me quite a fright

I was walking home from a moonlit stroll
Down by Dominican gate
When I saw this chap in a funny hat
And I thought I better wait

He was standing there without a care
At the door of the Superfry
With four cans of harp in a plastic bag
Just eating a mince steak pie

I approached the clown, (cause I'm from the town)
And we don't like trouble here
Plus I'd a bit of a thirst and the pub was shut
So I'd try to cadge a beer

"Alright young man, now what's the plan
With all this crazy gear
Your not wan of those aul killer clowns
And could you spare a lad a beer"

Well he munched for a bit on his pastry crust
(Which was actually chicken and ham)
Then reached inside his wee blue bag
And handed me a can

"Us killer clowns aren't all that bad
It started out as a bit of fun
Dressing up at Halloween
And scaring everyone"

Then someone had the bright idea
To carry a big sharpe knife
Now we've all been targeted
It's ruining my life

Party bookings have dried up
The kids don't want to know
Sean Graham turned down my offer of
A Red Sails one clown show

So I had no choice but to join the rest
And walk about in the dark
I've just been on the station road
The Warren and Lever Park

"Ach sir" said I, as he gave a sign
And his makeup started to drip
Finish your pie, dry your eye
And give your harp a sip

There's plenty of things a lad can do
Especially round these parts
The Anchor bar is full of clowns
Who are always getting starts

Grill The Burgers Slowly Folks

Grill the burgers slowly folks
Don't let the buggers burn
Wave two fingers at those guests
Who canny wait their turn

Piece your sausage twice or thrice
Rotate your silverware
Keep your meat on separate plates
And handle pork with care

Marinate your chicken breasts
If possible overnight
Prepare yourself for master chefs
You'll claim it's just not right

Pay no heed to those who shout
"Hey buddy up the flame"
Cause when their stuck on Armitage Shanks
It's you they'll surely blame

Dangerous Boys

Who's the biggest idiot
Farage or Donald Trump
I really can't decide whose face
Deserves a right good thump

Donald's getting all tooled up
And itching for a fight
Nigel's plans are so extreme
He's fallen off far right

A xenophobic opening
To sway the floating votes
Blame the pain on the immigrants
Drifting on their boats

For Mexicans and Muslims
Our Donald has no time
Add the blacks and they account
For all of U.S crime

Never mind the maniacs
The middle class white ones
Who run around in combat gear
Waving daddy's guns

From real estate to words of hate
Who's whispering in his ear
He's just a clown from funky town
It's his puppeteers I fear

And what about poor Nigel's
Well he's just a sad wee man
Who's heading off to Trumpville
To join Don's little klan

Narcoleptic Zombie Parents

I'm a narcoleptic zombie parent
Pupils hanging out my head
You'll find me creeping in the hallway
Howling for my precious bed

Limbs are moving, brain is dormant
Without the strength nor will to talk
Beaten, bruised and barely human
In the bowels of night I walk

Avoid temptation to console me
For tread I, a solemn path
Wide of eye the child tormentith
With a cooing torturous laugh

Bark of hound and creak of doorframe
Amplified a thousand times
Hold their whist as I approach them
Mumbling recurring rhymes

Mind transforming dark illusions
Barricade the goal I seek
The sanctuary of a small hotel room
Where perhaps I'll get some sleep

So if you meet me in the daylight
Don't let opinions be misled
I'm a narcoleptic zombie parent
Rehearsing for the walking dead

Here's Hoping

Here's hoping the Yankees will come to their senses
And Sponge Bob and Lightyear will lead the defences
On a spaceship I've made out of recycled plastic
Environment friendly and completely fantastic

Fairy bottles and toilet rolls
PlayStation joystick for controls
Wheels from the neighbours discarded old pram
Jars that my mum used to keep for the jam

Pieces of this, pieces of that
Bits of old carpet we'd kept for the cat
Before she was struck by a 53 bus
And scraped off the road with the minimum fuss

And buried outback in a bag in the ground
On a patch with a flower and a football sized mound
For there's always dirt left when you full in the hole
Kids use it now just to mark out the goal

But, back to the story and less bout the hump
I'm worried by candidates Clinton and Trump
And feel in the absence of rational though
Someone needs to question "is this all they've got?"

Could they not offer up just one brilliant mind
To promote the virtues of western mankind
Are they all born from cross burning gun wielding freaks
Come on America you've only three weeks

Clinton has dodgy tattooed on her heart
Donald is gradually falling apart
For his wandering, wrinkly locker room hands
Are groping the life from his leadership plans

But where are the options
Is this Salems lot?
Here's hoping this isn't
As good as they've got

The Latter Stages of Pregnancy

Time is of no relevance
In the latter stages of pregnancy
And attempts at humour best avoided

The role of he
Is tend to she
As fetcher, getter, carrier

It is advisable
Not to engage in conversations
Of a controversial nature

If the shelf needs moved
It is always best to move it immediately
It can always be put back

Lock photo albums away
And no your bum does not look big in this,
Unless that is you want it to

If you cut your finger
Under no circumstances
Mention it

Football has not been invented yet
Nor indeed has sport of any kind
The pub is closed

Sleep when you are told to sleep
There is never enough grass to mow
But mow it anyway

There is a method for hanging washing
You have not been taught it
Do not develop a new method

Attend all medical appointments
Thought offer no opinion, especially when asked,
For you are not the doctor

If she is hot, it is hot
If she is cold, it is cold
If she is hot and cold, it is your fault

Restless legs are not an indication
That she wants to go for a walk
But maybe you should, with the kids

Irrespective of how the saying goes
In this particular case
It did not take "two to tango"

Dinner is always lovely
Fast food is a viable alternative
Ice cream will help the baby

Shoulder rubs are free
There are no programmes on TV
That must be watched

You will experience a feeling
That is similar to vagrancy
Embrace the challenge comrades
"She's in the latter stages of pregnancy"

She's Back Into Her Jeans

Oh glory, now the day has come
She's seen it in her dreams
Young Donnacha has joined the clan
Spurred on by yelps and screams
Maternity dress is in the bin
For you don't know what it means
To see my lady strut about
In a pair of denim jeans

She's ditched the long black trousers
With expanding rubber band
And grabbed the Levi 501's
Into her twitchy hand
And like a peacock, feathers out
In front of me she'll stand
Theres a look of satisfaction
On this very lucky man

These last nine months have flown by
Or so I have been told
Attempts to younger up myself
Have left me feeling old
But when she's got the wranglers on
My babe I need to hold
Though the midwife in the Royal last week
Has said I need controlled

So now she's got the jeans back on
The journeys is complete
He's lovely little eyes and ears
Fingers toes and feet
He looks so cute in his baby suit
Especially when asleep
And mum has got her mojo back
She's dancing in the street

The Stresses of You Mother's

I've felt the pain of mother's
My sisters and the wife
Viewed the world through ladies eyes
Got a window to your life

I've stood in sheer frustration
By a freshly pine mopped floor
As three wee dirty buggers
Came running in the door

For as I'm in the garden
Mowing lawns and shifting earth
She's been in maternity
Eating fruit and giving birth

So all the household duties
Have befallen on to me
I've had to feed the hungry hoards
Breakfast, lunch and tea

Washing dishes, making beds
As every grubby face
Leaves their saucers, cups and plates
Lying round the place

Dirty socks and underwear
Are slowly piling high
The basket in the laundry room
Is reaching for the sky

Then the little one starts stirring
In the middle of the night
Climbs in bed beside me
To escape his fears and fright

So now I'm looking knackered
My skin is old and grey
The wrinkles on my forehead
Do multiply each day

But all these woe's and worries
Chasing Ellen and her brothers
Have offered me the chance to feel
The stresses of you mother's

Roller Coaster

365 of them
Yet I can't recall a single day
One roller coaster on top of another roller coaster
Meet an intercity train coming the other way

A white knuckle ride on a planet that kept on spinning
Even when our lives wanted to stop and scream
"Choose someone else, we want to get off
This isn't part of the American Dream"

But that lottery middle finger from the sky is pointing at us
And hospital corridors all look, smell and sound alike
The monitors don't stop monitoring
Just because the curtains close at night

Life can't always be predicted
Surprise is surely part of the eventual outcome
If not, our worlds would still be black and white
And roller coasters wouldn't be such fun

Frampton

A force that can unite us
With all cultures, race and creed
Cheering on a Belfast lad
Sure this is what we need

Singing, dancing, having fun
Let the bigots all take heed
This is integrated life
And this is what we need

In Gaelic, Soccer, Rugby tops
To America they speed
To cheer this guy from Tiger's Bay
This must be what we need?

With skilled determination
And a focus to achieve
He's building bridges in our land
Now this is what we need

So I thank you sir for what you do
And your fame is guaranteed
A million like Carl Frampton
This is what we need

People Die

People die
And life is often hard to understand
Ripples of emotion wash against our skin
For youth was never quite as we did plan

Still no nearer than to that which we recall
This race to adulthood was so appealing
We failed consistently to touch the beauty of it all
And lay in tears just staring at the ceiling

Desensitised to yet another dark atrocity
As fundamentalist and infidel collide
While others stand aghast with hand to face
We exposed do take it in our stride

When bombs go off
People die
Homes become graveyards
And children cry

Arsne Wenger's Long Zip Coat

Is it a dream or a forlorn hope
That I could one day own a coat
Like Arsne wears when on the line
Long zipped, blue and mighty fine

His beaming face he cannot hide
With big bald Bouldy by his side
In caterpillar, puffa cloak
Oh what a fashion conscious bloke

But what is this, he looks perplexed
His beady eyes appear quite vexed
When zipped up tightly to his throat
Alas the fastener he has broke

By endless tugging at the brass
He's jammed it tightly, hard and fast
And while the ball is still in play
Poor Wenger's plight is au contraire

With giggles rising from the bench
The silver clasp he tries to wrench
Spins around and scowls at those
Who dared pass comment on his clothes

Champions league or FA Cup
You can't deny this French mans pluck
To stand alone and take the flack
In his long zipped puffa anorak

The Demons Of Saturday Night

I'm slowly beginning to master
The demons of Saturday night
Readjusting my senses and vision
Getting my swollen head right

The feeling is gradually finding
It's path to the tips of my toes
I've shivered and shook all through Sunday
And wallowed in pity and woes

To the bathroom I've ran for salvation
From the rumbling toxic revenge
Prayed for a temporary cessation
And the watery outlook to change

The children had all been persuaded
To vacate the house for the day
Mum told them they had to stay quiet
And keep out of poor daddy's way

I've been to the shop for refreshments
Ice lollies and crisps have been bought
Tried quite a varied concoction
Of remedies, both cold and hot

But time is the only great healer
It cannot be rushed or cajoled
Tricked or mislead to move faster
Flummoxed, bamboozled or fooled

But I'm slowly beginning to master
The demons of Saturday night
My movements are currently settled
And the forecast is looking quite bright

Socialists Come Ye Assemble

Socialists come ye assemble
For the fascists are gathering nigh
In suits tailor made in Westminster
The new Labour vultures fly high

Stand aside are their cries from the chambers
Which invokes such a traitorous stench
Supporting the Tory agenda
From the ranks of a shadowy bench

So they saddled a Tony Blair posse
A political lynching was sought
With Jeremy's face on the poster
The leader who wouldn't be bought

Ignoring the calls of their members
On a scurrilous coup they embark
May their union cards lie in the embers
As the red flame burns bright in the dark

So socialists come ye assemble
The Fascists are now close at hand
A strong opposition is needed
With Jeremy Corbyn we stand

Robbie Brady's Babies

It's all a game of ifs and maybe's
But she wants Robbie Brady's babies
Said, she'd swap her new Mercedes
Or ply him full of stout and bailey's

So I'm a bloke and not a lady
And the concept may sound shady
But when he scored the place went crazy
We all proclaimed "we want his baby"

Alas the French have once again
Flushed Irish dreams right down the drain
But sitting here in wind and rain
She says "I still want Robbies wain"

I tell her "love the game is gone"
It's time for us to all move on
But she is looking all forlorn
Stating, she still wants his spawn

"Robbie's Irish through and through
With curly hair and eyes of blue
Not old and wrinkly just like you
I'll bet he has a bob or two"

"Relax" says I "and calm your jets
Ok the lad has found the nets
His skin ain't dulled by cigarettes
He's not weighed down with bills and debts

From Galway town to Malahide
There's young girls, old girls, going wild
Those at home and those exiled
Who want a Robbie Brady child

My Granny Was A Murphy

My granny was a Murphy
I heard my father say
She travelled here to England
On her twenty first birthday
Met a bloke from Liverpool
And married him in May
Settled down in Lancashire
Just north of Morecambe Bay

I've always thought I'm English
That's what my passport said
I've dreamed of winning World Cup's
While lying on my bed
But now I'm not so certain
Doubts rushing through my head
This Brexit vote on Thursday night
Has filled my heart with dread

I don't believe in UKIP
With their politics of hate
Michael Gove's right wing assault
On our ailing welfare state
Boris Johnston's lust for power
And backstabbing of his mate
Economic suicide
With rising interest rate

This Farage suited racism
Don't hold no ground with me
A European state of mind
Is the vision that I see
So what could be my options
Where can the answer be
Perhaps an Irish passport
Like my granny Rose Murphy

What About Those Boys In Green

What about the boys in green
God bless the Pope, then save the Queen
The greatest party ever seen
The stuff of every Irish dream

Arlene and Marty in the stands
Sharing jokes and holding hands
Dancing girls and marching bands
A melting pot of football fans

The President and his First Lady
Niall Maginn and Robbie Brady
Chances slim and looking shady
You never know, just maybe baby

Fuelled up on finest Beaujolais
The Shinners and the UDA
Join forces while the games in play
As Wales and France stand in the way

They've lifted bottles from the street
Downed herds of processed burger meat
Serenaded girls they meet
And helped young children get to sleep

So what about those boys in green
We're still all here, two weeks it's been
Livers starting now to scream
And credit union looking mean

Sleep Deprivation

This sleep deprivation's a funny old thing
It's messing around with my head
I'm out of my body and out of my mind
But mostly I'm out of my bed

I've lost the incentive, the get up and go
The spark has most nearly gone out
Resisting the prospect of running away
Choosing instead just to shout

My colleagues at work are avoiding my stare
My family are staying outside
People who see me are crossing the road
Children are starting to hide

My poor wife is now in a similar state
We're passing like ships in the night
Donnacha's feeding like Horace the hound
The beautiful greedy wee mite

My Babe, The Buggy and A Mobile Phone

Good morning world I'm a modern man
Strutting proudly with my pram
Steady pace no need for speed
Displaying the fruits of my virile seed

Stand aside for here I am
Middle aged bloke with a Graco pram
Big smug grin, couldn't be more happy
Up to my oxters in toxic nappy

Down the park or up the street
Snow white nikes upon my feet
Ready for action like a Belgrave harrier
Two arms free in my Chicco carrier

A lifetimes joy for three minutes of fun
Recording memories for everyone
Toddling along in a world of my own
My babe, the buggy and a mobile phone

Beer Bottles In The Sky
(Read to the tune of ghost riders in the sky)

A hooligan from Blighty's shores
Went with his mates to France
Got tanked up in an Irish bar
Then did a merry dance
And as he waved his little flag around
There gathered quite a crowd
The way he sang God Save The Queen
Must make her highness proud

The French police could take no more
And drew their wooden bats
They weighed into the English lads
And herded them like rats
Fred Perry shirts and trilby hats
Were scattered as they ran
These punters are just hooligans
Not genuine football fans

So all around the continent
We ask the question why
When Blighty's boys go on the road
The bottles start to fly
In every corner of the globe
Their countries flag they shame
And spoil it for the rest of us
Who love the beautiful game

We all knew it would happen
So why should we complain
They've done it out in Germany
And parts of southern Spain
It's called the bulldog spirit
They've seen it on the news
So when they see a foreigner
They spread their right wing views

Yippee ki yay, for England they'll die
Beer bottles, flying in the sky

Dodgy Dave

I doff my cap to Dennis
A man who stood his ground
And called young David dodgy
For pocketing mums pound

As all around old blighty
Folks scrape to stay afloat
His dough is in the Caymans
In an off shore money boat

Two hundred thousand greenbacks
In a "best boy" birthday card
Just a little present
To help when times get hard

Let's not forget the handout
He got from dear old dad
And the hundred grand per annum
As he rents his London pad

But it normal common practice
Called financial enterprise
To move your cash around a bit
In case the old dear dies

Well I don't believe you David
Nor that dodgy Osbourne bloke
But the fact that people vote for you
Is the biggest bloody joke

PLAYA

You tell me the venue,
The time and the place
And I'll fail to assemble
A name to a face

With an awkward acceptance
I'll acknowledge defeat
As you shuffle embarrassed
Then stare at your feet

For I had consigned it
To a drunken affair
Devoid of commitment
Feelings or care

Just another bland fling
To top off the night
A takeaway special
With a spicy wee bite

I didn't expect it
To lead anywhere
That you would have feelings
Emotions or care

Let alone think
We would meet up again
For I wasn't seeking
A fling with a brain

So once again tell me
The time and the place
For I'm sure I can put back
That smile on your face

I'll get us a drink
As you ditch your mate
She's cramping our style
And you've got a date!

Squat Life

I lived in a squat when I was just eighteen
Not far from Hackney marsh
We'd a cement floor and a wrought iron door
And life at times was harsh

The Pembury estate was my address
At the top of old Mare street
A two bed flat in a grey tower block
With a mattress on to sleep

On a Monday night in the local bar
The Three Sisters was its name
I was throwing arrows at the board
When a bloke offered me a game

It was the landlord of the pub
And I played just like a dream
He offered me a rake of drink
If I'd join the local team

So I threw for him in the London league
But I had to use his flights
Union Jacks in an Irish pub
Just didn't sit quite right

An argument did then ensue
Kingsland Road was the place
When I won a game with a double ten
And they didn't like my face

In haste I packed my arrows up
And headed for the door
But left the landlords Union flights
Scattered on the floor

I boxed meat for a man with a dodgy tash
In a freezer at Turn Pike Lane
We met for our wages in The Rising Sun
And we never asked his name

Was glassed by a lad in the National
In Kilburn, one Friday night
At the time I think I laughed him off
Then offered him a fight

He lunged at me and raised his fist
As I appeased him with a jar
And told him I was not the bloke
Who pushed him at the bar

A country lad who lived with us
Was mugged for his brass in the tower
So he said he'd had enough of life
For the shit had gone too far

He'd a rake of kids to feed at home
And I use to help him write
But he knew they'd think he'd drank it all
And he couldn't take the shite

I lived in a squat when I was just eighteen
Neath London's shining lights
I've thrown darts in the London league
And been in bar room fights

But They Didn't Have A Seven

I've always had a keen eye
For a brown suede desert boot
And I guess, I was bout fourteen
When this craving first took root

It was in the town of Coleraine
As I waited patiently
For a girl from the local Convent
To share a cup of tea

I'd asked myself the question
"Sure what have I to lose?"
As I waded through the loafers
And shiny patent shoes

But I knew she wasn't coming
When the clock strayed well past four
And with each swish I raised my eyes
Towards the sliding door

So my self esteem I packed away
Inside my pencil case
As I felt a fresh young pimple
Give birth upon my face

What could I do to ease the pain
In this brogue retailing heaven
I tried a pair Chelsea boots
But they didn't have a seven

Someone's Gone And Ate My Flake

Call it schoolboy error
Or an obvious mistake
For I left it in the cupboard
By the fruit and almond cake

Stuck behind the Nutty Crust
I'd planned it for tea break
But an evil eye had spied my treat
And swiped it like a snake

So now I'm left dejected
With a rumbling bellyache
For as I worked my nine to five
Someone nicked my flake

I Think I Know Your Face

There's a young fella from Lurgan
I think I know his face
I've seen him in the papers
And all over the place

He often on the telly
Parading with the stars
Or holding cheques on Facebook
From local shops and bars

I hear he's got a fan club
Not in English but in Greek
Promoting Downs Awareness
From the top of William Street

Some people say " he's special"
But we just call him Jay
I think he speaks to Samaras
Every single day

He's got an extra Chromosome
So whats that all about
Like, does he sit in silence?
Will he not run about?

Will I have to nurse him
If he gets sick at night?
Can he go to school each day?
Please tell me, is that right?

Will he be a lonely child?
Will he have no friends?
Can he go on holidays?
This nightmare never ends

He has an extra Chromosome
And loves to run about
If you've seen him at a Celtic match
You'll know he loves to shout

And yes he'll need your comfort
If at night his tummy's sore
But don't you fear, you'll miss him
When he runs through the school door

Of course he's not a lonely child
His friends are far and wide
Lurgan, Athens, Belfast
And all along the Clyde

Ah now I get the message
He's just like any child
Some days he's warm and loving
But mostly he's just wild!

School Run

So I can't find my car keys
And he's sitting on the stairs
I'm like, yeah yeah yeah your shoes
As if he even cares

Then I don't tie the laces
Like the laces should be tied
The way the cool kids have them
Hidden in the side

He says I'm not a baby
He'll do it on his own
As I find the mislaid car keys
Now where's my mobile phone

The phone is in the pocket
Of the coat I always wear
The child is tying laces
While sitting on the stair

The keys, just for safekeeping
I've put into the door
School bag, lunch included
Is resting on the floor

Football after school today
You owe PC three pound
Breakfast dishes, underwear
Scattered on the ground

Face and teeth completed
Carnage in the sink
Knickers lifted, pocket change
That's everything I think

I swear I'll do things differently
Implement a rule
To ease the stress and tension
Of the daily run to school

Dick Turpin Wore A Mask

By two whole pounds and thirteen pence
My limit did exceed
As Shylock, now the bankers come
Upon my flesh to feed
"Are you the holder of this card
The heartless beast does ask
Then states the bloody obvious,
Dick Turpin wore a mask

There'll be a fine of fifteen pounds
For you broke what was agreed
And another twelve for the overdraft
As he rubs his hands with greed
Then he comes all sympathetic
Says he's got a thankless task
I remind him that we bailed them out
Dick Turpin wore a mask

Then patronisingly enquires
"Will we pay if off today
Sort this little issue out"
To get me on my way
I tell him he has not the right
In my predicament to bask
That although he was a robber
Dick Turpin wore a mask

When the global Lehman Brothers
Brought the banking system down
Governments chose to save them
But let the people drown
So when your sitting in the street
Supping cold tea from a flask
Remember that you saw their face
Cause Dick Turpin wore a mask

God Save Our Leslie Grantham

God save their Leslie Grantham
Let them sing it in the stands
No need to contact Van the man
Or any trendy bands

They don't want any Teenage Kicks
Or Barry's "Derry air"
They won't stand still for Brown Eyed Girl
In Larne or Ballyclare

I like the thought of SLF
Or Ash's "Girl From Mars"
Ringing out before the match
In Belfast's clubs and bars

But the fans seem quite divided
On what they ought to do
Some even mentioned Snow Patrol
And Bono from U2

So save their Leslie Grantham
Let it ring from every mouth
And kids who don't feel welcome
Will represent the South

An Atheist Walks Into A Bar

An atheist walked into a Belfast bar
Earlier this year
Took off his coat and cleared his throat
Then softly whispered "beer"

I have but only two requests
From those assembled here
Refreshment and enlightenment,
Now who will volunteer

A Pastor from the local church
Was protesting near bye
At a play depicting nudity
When he heard the atheist cry

He thrust a pamphlet in his hand
And stared him in the eye
Repent forth hence or ye shall burn,
Until the day you die

The atheist laughed and shook his head
Then wished the pastor well
In no way re-enlightened
By the eternal threat of hell

A Priest was taking delivery
Of some fresh Communion wine
When he heard the atheist in the bar
And thought " this poor soul's mine"

Now son your lack of faith in God
Is the curse of modern time
Turn your back on worldly goods
And I'm sure you'll be just fine

Again the atheist shook his head
As he walked him to the door
So you'll sell the Vatican's precious art
And donate them to the poor?

"Will no one save my lost belief?"
The atheist did shout
Just as a Rabbi passed the pub
And asked " what's this about?"

"My friend you say you've lost your way
Come join the chosen tribe
We've a lovely country in the sun
And the yanks are on our side"

The atheist then waved his hand
"Alas I must decline,
For that countries hands are drenched in blood
From the streets of Palestine

The atheist then grabbed his coat
And finished off his drink
"There's little here that I've heard today
To change the way I think"

Then he waved goodbye and left the bar
Heading off along the street
When he walked in the path of a speeding car
Which knocked him off his feet

A nurse woke him up in a hospital bed
With his left leg in a sling
Cuts and bruises on his head
And he couldn't mind a thing

"An angel's watching over you
For there's not much damage done"
"Your right" the atheist did reply
"But I wish I knew which one"

The Bastard Cats of Donal Walsh

The bastard cats of Donal Walsh
Have gathered on my shed
They gaze on me with hungry stare
Awaiting to be fed

A multicoloured feline fest
Unfolds outside my back
Ginger Tom and tortious shell
Ghostly white and black

Each an offspring of the night
Who resemble one another
They share their fathers lustful traits
And a weather beaten mother

No royal line of privilege here
And scant respect for age
It's one for all and all for one
When they venture through the hedge

Like prairie beasts they roam the night
With deathly piecing cries
These bastard cats of Donal Walsh
I'm growing to despise

Foreign Television Remote Control Fiasco

I'm sitting here blankly in a bit of a hole
Holding on to a foreign television control
The concept is generally that which I know
However the bloody thing just will not go

It's a 42 inch flat screen systemised set
But I haven't quite managed the control etiquette,
I've sampled the vino with a preference for red
And probably should have retired to my bed

But the want to extend till the tiny wee hours
And the early insistence to depart from the bars
Has resulted in one slowly getting distressed
With the lack of response from each symbol I press

I'm starting to panic and questioning "why"
When faced with a option of HDMI
Various menus, adjustment in size
Consistently failing to answer my cries

While there's flashing and opening on the adjacent shelf
With gadgets and gizmos moving all by themselves
I call to the hostess to get them involved
And with a tap on the handset all was resolved

She raises her eyes and then refills my glass
Relieved that my moment of panic has passed
Normal service resumed just in time for my show
No more foreign television remote control fiasco

A Puppy Is Not Just For Christmas, It's Forever

Behind every door there's a trace of urine
Dispatched by a puppy or a displaced feline
And a constant echo of a childish "not mine"
Requiring a mop from me

As the crack of dawn peeps through the curtain
There's one thing that I know for certain
That my smelling sense will soon be hurting
And I'll need to get the mop

All day she scratches at the door
And leaves wee jobbies on the floor
That others simply do ignore
I'll go and get the mop

She snaps at those who bend their nose
And bites on exposed fathers toes
And pisses everywhere she goes
I'll need a second mop

Shouting At Kids On A Rainy Morn

Overweight kids battle across once green plains
Stuffing oversized bacon baps in unwashed faces
Senses dulled by over indulgence on call of duty number 9,
But they are mine

They are my Ronaldo's, my Jennings, my Dixie Deans
My Stapleton's, Ian Rush, my Robbie Keane's
And I their Ferguson, their big Jock Steins
For this is the stuff of boyhood dreams

Here, where history meets the new
This cabin with the dodgy loo
Those ones who are the chosen few
They wear the red, the green, the blue

For these are my Maradona's
Best, Doherty and Pele
The tricks, the flicks, the Belfast Tele
YouTube cameras at the ready

Shouting at kids on a rainy morn
We breath the highs, the lows, the breaks
The crossbar ping, the time it takes
For him and all those damned mistakes

My Jinxy Johnstone's, and dear Gazza
My Larssons, my Eric Cantona
My Brady, my oh ah Paul McGrath
That special one, je ne sais quoi

Scumbag Christmas

Sitting here I can but think
Of takeaway cartons in the sink
Broken toys from Poundland city
Bought without thought and pretty shitty
Cardboard heaven in the yard
"I'd put it in the bin, but you see I'm hard"

So much to do so little time
Full as a tit on Buckfast wine
Spark a fag and scratch my balls
Tinsel falling from the walls
Out the kids go, just for a while
Quality street and jeremy kyle,

Onesie on, out to chippy
Bring my gown its getting nippy,
Battered lads and fish to go
Festive edition of The One Show
Bottle of vodka, beans on toast
Boxing Day, Racing Post

See in New Year with a midnight snog
Throw my guts up in the bog
Swear I'll never drink again
Lose my door key, what's my name?
Stagger home in the crisp white snow
It's a scumbag Christmas, ho ho ho

Blood

My blood is crimson red upon the stone
It darkens to a deathly charcoal stain
Should I have cause to bleed in Paris or Beirut
My deep red blood still flows the very same

My blood is warm and often slow to cease
As fever it engulf's each new embrace
Reflected in the stare of every child
Regardless of the colour of their face

My blood erupts when stripped from pumping vein
High in sky or as young lovers meet
Torn from heart with little thought of care
Speckled black on lonely dusty street

My blood is now forever on their hands
As too, my flame scotched flesh and twisted bone
Those who came like Devils in the night
And they who turn their countries into stone

Some May Turn To Prayer

Some may turn to prayer
When struggles they may face
Offer up some quiet thoughts
From a dark and lonely place
Call on Saints and Prophets
To find some peace and grace
Seek a spiritual retreat
In His loving safe embrace

Some may turn to prayer
And thank the Lord each day
For every breath that they inhale
To help them on their way
Seek a friend to hold their hand
When life has gone astray
A branch that reaches out to them
That keeps the fear at bay

Call on He who rests your heart
To help attend your needs
Gather round you faithful friends
Cards and rosary beads
Banish negativity
On which this cancer feeds
Together strength will be your guide
Along the path He leads

The Bus Driver

Gan drive us home Mike
And dinny make a fuss
I've got myself a window seat
On this here Ulsterbus
I wouldn't whistle at the back
Spit or swear or cuss
Sure bring thon Arlene if you like
But she's an aul sour puss

Gan drive us home Mike
And give us all your news
Don't you support Glentoran
Or could it be the blues
I'll swallow up ma chewing gum
Then it won't get on your shoes
You can leave us at the roundabout
Which ever stop you choose

Gan drive us home Mike
My ma's got on the tea
She likes that lad Frank Mitchell
The one on UTV
I think it's fish and chips tonight
Hold the mushy pea
You can park the bus around the back
Just say that your with me

"You'll get no lift home Marty lad
I'm calling it a night
So get yourself to Halfords
And buy a bloody bike"
You should have been more nice to me
And said that I was right
That Gerry Kelly on The View
Gave me quite a fright

Ach gan drive us hame Mike
I'll use ma Derry charm
Gerry's not a bad bloke
He didn't mean no harm
My ma will set an extra place
She keeps the spare room warm
I wouldn't want to have to break
Or sorry, twist your arm

Sibling Rivalry

She cracked the pencil lead
Against her brother's head
Fathers eyes were filled with dread
In fear the boy could well be dead
But he did scream aloud instead
Her face went pink with blotchy red
Then she was sent to early bed
Unfed
As he crunched on his toasted bread

The Revolving Door Of Hypocrites

With the hand of history resting on their shoulder
And feet still blistering from those summer walks
The men in grey are looking so much older
As they entertained another round of talks

With Arlene left to steer this new Titanic
And keep the rogues and renegade's at bay
She didn't see the ice berg in the distance
Too busy chasing butterflies away

The British parliamentary lads and lassies
When Nigel stuck his arm up in the air
Sighed and quickly sought another question
To demonstrate they really couldn't care

The revolving door of bitter politicians
Hypocrites who still receive full pay
While they are shouting "give us preconditions"
Our services are starting to decay

Lament Of The Last Man Standing

Go on ye boy, good man your da
You stuck the pace to get this far
As all around you, soldiers fell
And drifted into spinning hell

Stood your ground and kept your seat
When others melted in the heat
Hunched bodies strewn cross the floor
Nauseous sighs and stuttered snore

You sit in victory on your throne
O're lesser men who ventured home
And stumbled off into the night
Without the stomach for the fight

But last sips seldom taste as fresh
As dawn peeps through the smoke stained mesh
Then strain your eye to fix a stare
At all your friends who are not there

Battle's ensue within your head
Of names, liaisons, laughter, bed
Chronologies of who went where
That girl you spoke with on the stair

Resigned you grapple for your coat
From drunken stranger drenched in boke
Quick check the pocket for your keys
Then curse missed opportunities

What Did You Do In The 80's Dad?

What did you do in the 80's dad?
He looked up at me and said
His interest now ignited
By a book his teacher read
An age when all around the globe
Demands for change rang out
We dandered up and down the prom
And sort of, hung about

As riots lit the skies at night
And bricks and bottles flew
I spiked my hair with my mothers spray
Then chased a girl or two
Our conversations centred on
Young Zammo, from Grange Hill
The only time we saw a cop
Was when we watched The Bill

Yeh things began to change a bit
from 1982
Life was less in black and white
And more red, white and blue
Maybe I was growing up
Becoming more in tune
To ethical dilemmas
Beyond the living room

Of rights to civil liberties
No matter race or creed
Sexual persuasions
Or how you choose to breed
I looked to those who questioned
Those rules once set in stone
And felt affiliation
With their socialistic tone

I started reading history
Bought a Billy Bragg EP
Studied documentary's
On Channel 4 TV
The bright lights of old Belfast
Summoned me forth haste
So I packed up all my politics
And some Clearsil for my face

I continued with my studies
And like those I chanced to meet
Priorities were having fun
And something warm to eat
While nurturing our friendships
We learnt to understand
Ignorance is our enemy
In this great wee piece of land

So what did I do in the 80's
Well, I learnt the greatest rule
To turn your back on difference
Are the actions of the fool

Trip To Clones 1997

As heavy heads left feather beds
The mini bus arrived
Six of us with plastic bags
Joined the rest inside

Few words were spoke for fear of boke
As we took our seat within
Till the rasp of open tin of harp
Signalled supping to begin

The early morning worshippers
Who passed the transit van
Were met with " what about ye high"
And the raising of a can

Then Russell Cellars carry outs
We quickly did dispatch
And signalled for the driver to
"Girl, take us tae the match"

With Doire shirts all freshly ironed
Tucked into stone washed denim
We planned to pick the tickets up
In the Tower bar at eleven

"Hats, scarfs, and headbands"
Did rise above the throng
As from a local hostelry
There blared a rebel song

A cavalcade of Northern plates
All sought a place to park
We ditched the driver and the bus
And made our disembark

Got a sausage bap from a red faced guy
Whose hair was thick and greasy
A pleasant bloke who took the joke
And said " feck lads go easy"

Along the street from pub to pub
By the time we reached St Tiernach's
We all were looking worse for wear
And talking utter bollocks

The game I think we lost that day
But I couldn't say the score
I was just glad I could walk and talk
When I reached my bedroom door

Oh it's hard to beat the aul GAA
On a summers afternoon
Hand to toe or clash of ash
It sure does lift the gloom

Protect

Wrap your arm around me dad
Protect me through the night
Tell my dreams to bring me joy
And I will be alright

Hold my hand if I should fall
Speak words that ease my pain
Gently wipe away my tear
Then help me run again

Be the rock below my feet
When strangers break my heart
Ease the pieces back in place
If I should fall apart

Answer, should I call on you
When life has gone array
See behind the mask I wear
Protect me every day

Peculiar Testicular Manoeuvre

A friend who I've got through the social arcade
Advised of a recent discovery he made
That put all his plans, for a while in the shade
And left him at the mercy of the ball doctors blade

For one day, as he merrily rummaged around
Oblivious to every slight murmur and sound
A rather peculiar blemish he found
Resembling that like a little dark mound

My mate, a good man of some artistic class
Stood there, struck in silence, in front of the glass
And knowing that he could not just let this pass
Dropped his blue Levi's right down by his ass

A nervous inspection confirmed his worst fear
Could this the product of too many beer
He drew in a breath and then battled a tear
And called in the family that he holds so dear

The doctors fixed camera's and probes to a stick
And said " right then lad, let's look in your dick"
"Now just you relax, for you'll feel a small prick"
"I'll try and be merciful, painless and quick"

They must have been hoking for near half the day
Then up sprung the surgeon and stood back away
Deflected the complements on his display
And said "don't touch that wee scrotum till well after May"

Now raving and dancing is out for our groover
And woe betide him should he go near the Hoover
But he's got his smile back and his sack is much smoother
Since he had his peculiar testicular manoeuvre

The Wake

The production of the tea
And short bread biscuits
Intermingled with the old favourite
The Jacobs fig roll
Brought the inevitable question
"Did we ever find out who actually did
put the figs in the fig rolls"
We chuckle then adjust the atmosphere accordingly

Muffled silence is broken
By the reprimanding of someone's Uncle
Who made in inexcusable decision
To rest his "Rosy Lee"
On the the old mans mahogany box
Again we chuckle,
He raises his eyebrows apologetically
She shakes her head despairingly

We are shuffled closer to the floor
To provide suitable seated accommodation
To an elderly aunt
Who smells of flowers
Carpet space from this point becomes precious.
Even those of questionable stature
Appear like giants from where we now kneel

Staring at a picture of my uncle on the wall
As he casts his eye over those assembled
I ponder his opinion of the gathering,
Then distracted by what I
At the time deemed inappropriate laughter,
His brothers recall their memories
When I return my gaze to the photograph,
I swear he is smiling

I'll Shout For Revolution

I'll shout for revolution
From the comfort of my chair
Curse the blind hypocrisy
Of those who claim to care
For countries left in ruins
From the bombs of Bush and Blair
Then question their intentions
And the reason they were there

I'll shout for revolution
From behind my garden gate
At divide and conquer attitude's
And their politics of hate
They'll stitch us up for sure this time
On an ageing welfare state
That needs a blood transfusion
Though gets a four year wait

I'll shout for revolution
And wave my toasted bread
As fears stoked up of days long gone
Leave our futures all but dead
This prehistoric bigotry
Banging in their head
Beats old sectarian rhetoric
That fills my heart with dread

I'll shout for revolution
From the dusty wooden seat
Though fear that few are listening
Our insurrection's beat
For those who pull the puppet strings
Won't entertain defeat
Their fighting fires on several fronts
And the kitchens full of heat

I Know I Met You On The Slow Boat To Scouseville

Take the slow boat back across
You'll save yourself some dough
Get a seat beside the bar
And off to sleep you go

Leaves Belfast port at half past ten
And takes about nine hours
Lorry drivers fancy it
And blokes who export cars

Hairy unwashed student types
Are curled up on the floor
In combat coats and DM boots
And jeans all bleached and tore

So I packed up my belongings
My jumpers and my smalls
In a bag I got in JJB
Beside the cheap footballs

Bought my ticket, grabbed a pew
On a row of seats of three
Paid a quid for a bag of crisps
Then two for a cup of tea

Seemed to look around a lot
For half and hour or more
Went to the bog, then changed my mind
As I couldn't lock the door

Bobbed around for quite a bit
First left and then to the right
The engines made a thunderous roar
As we sailed into the night

No WiFi then, nor Sky TV
To pacify the brain
Just left to right, right to left
Again, again, again

I craved a liquid sedative
A quiet pint to help me sleep
Picked a stool that was screwed down tight
So I wouldn't lose my feet

I had a drink to help me rest
Then one for company
Should have stopped at number two
But headed on to three

Four went by without a thought
Five and six were tough
I must have choked on a bit of boke
For the sea was mighty rough

About this time I saw you both
As you blended into one
You looked like a lass who liked a glass
And a bit of harmless fun

I sauntered ore to where you sat

Like a saddle soar John Wayne
You rolled your eyes and mumbled that
"You should have got the plane"
Now never one to give up hope
Or hold my feelings back
I offered you my company
Alcohol and crac

Well I quickly went from bad to worse
As I downed seven and eight
The look you threw at number nine
Was filled with utter hate

Maybe it was what I said
Or the atmosphere was wrong
Probably was number ten
As I did the Birdie Song

Well I never saw that lass again
And I guess I never will
But theres no such thing as a quiet pint
On that slow boat to Scouseville

There Will Always Be Some

There will always be some
Who miss the comfortable feel
Of dark cold burning steel
Crack of bone, turn of heel
Coffin stand, mothers kneel
Clergy call for need to heal
Media seeking politicians appeal
For calm to try and save the deal
When we all know the truth is real

There will always be some
Who seek to use this latest threat
To call in some historical debt
And while never letting us forget
Will say it is with some regret
They must withdraw from this duet
As with a trembling cigarette
Drenched with camera lit sweat
They pause the small black peace cassette

Refugees

Hopeless souls on hungry sea
They come to us, these refugees
With babes in arms on bended knee
As tyranny and war they flee

In coffin ships upon the wave
The mercy of the deep they brave
As lowered to their watery grave
Outstretched hands our lives do crave

Loaded up and pushed adrift
With only that which they could lift
Lost children through the bodies sift
Survival is their greatest gift

I watched a father raise his young
And beg the sanctuary of one
Who stood behind a loaded gun
Some cover from the burning sun

So to the ocean floor they ease
From flowing tears and endless pleas
And gently floating on the breeze
The ghosts of all our refugees

The Great Oak

There stands within my garden
A ten year old oak tree
We planted it together
When my son was about three

Through every leaf it carries
The sun shines through each day
The branches make the light reflect
In such a magic way

No beam is like another
Nor shadow look alike
It stretches out to touch the sky
From break of day till night

I watch it's different colours
From the comfort of my chair
It brings a sense of peaceful still
As it dances in the air

I took a saw the other day
For its shape did not comply
My son looked up from his PS4
And simply asked me "why"

"Just let the branches find their way
And the leaves will come and go
The path this tree will choose to take
Not one of us will know"

Waste

In a second life stopped
And everything that seemed important ceased
Every grudge and bitter thought was washed away
All that I despised was now released

Words that I had spoken in anger are now forgotten
Scars I bare upon my skin all heal
In war, insurrection, revolution, oppression I have lost heart
I cannot myself feel

There is no sound, no rain,
No sun, no air, for which I can complain
I cannot breathe, I have no weight within my core
From this point I shall not live again

Then he is found and tears fill the silence
Strangers gather round and comfort us
I have never felt so hollow and so dead
Now I shall replace the waste within my head

The Passing Of The Night

By the window pane she sits
In silence as the big arm ticks
And moth against the lamplight flits
The passing of the night

With shadow cast on gable wall
The beam from passing car does crawl
As in her mind she does recall
The passing of the night

Till they return she shall not rest
With bible clutched tight to her breast
She keeps her fears for them suppressed
Through the passing of the night

Then hurried step in lashing rain
She hears the lock and slip of chain
And peace upon her heart again
She passes through the night

Messages

My father used to ask me
When I was just a lad
To join him for a Sunday drive
Along the promenade

He'd say he had some messages
To call with Vincent Roughan
But I knew it was a chance for us
To spend time on our own

He'd pack a box of envelopes
In the back seat of the car
Tell my mum that we " were off"
And "We'd be about an hour"

From Old Coach Road to Lever Park
A dozen homes or more
He'd pull the car beside the kerb
And head towards the door

Every time he'd bring with him
A box of envelopes
Then stand with, Leo, Ray or John
And exchange several jokes

Heathmount on to Harryville
We'd call with Mrs Kerr
She always had a smiling face
And offered up a prayer

94

Seafield Park, Coleraine Road
Burnside and then the Strand
He'd call at nearly twenty homes
With the wee box in his hand

The sun was always setting
When we reached the promenade
Morrelli's was the final stop
And I'd stare up at my dad

The back seat was now empty
And we would head back home
My dad had done his messages
And I had earned a cone

Natures Living Room

Sitting in the drizzle in Lurgan Park
On a bench that is damp with rain
The uncomfortable touch of a soggy slack
As I question my judgement again

To leave the house with no waterproof coat
More in hope than expectation
Now I sit in the shade of a great oak tree
And await the wet cessation

Feathers fly as the ripples fall
On the crest of the silvery bed
Each stake their claim upon the grass
To the crumbled remains of bread

And still the walkers lead their dogs
In contempt at the bruised grey skies
Still the swing does gently rock
In time with the children's cries

Sitting in the drizzle in Lurgan Park
On a Monday afternoon
Is there anywhere finer in this whole world
Than natures living room

Problem Solved

The commissions made it's ruling
In the soaring summer heat
Alas the poor old brethren
Can't walk the Ardoyne street

But I may have the solution
To unite community
And give an unexpected boost
To a flat economy

Put a toll before the shops
An another on the crum
Charge a fiver through the gate
And make a tidy sum

Join the credit union
Invest the bandsman's dough
With all the marches in July
You'll see the savings grow

And when the seasons over
And the drums no longer play
Take you money from the bank
And have a street party!!

I Never Did Quite Get The Offside Rule

I stood there with the other condemned pupils at our school
Waiting for someone to point and say we'll take that fool
And though they stuck me at the back which wasn't all that cool
I never really got to grips with that bloody offside rule

"So run that by me once again, I'm playing him onside?"
Then I in vain reflect the blame as my shame I tried to hide
"It's second phase, he's not in play, the ball was going wide"
"You can't be offside from a throw" the captain then replied

"Move up, don't drop, just stay in line" the older ones would
shout
"And when you hear me give the sign get everybody out"
"Mark that big lad with the hair, don't let him run about
Watch him close, he's a slippy wan he's like a flamin trout"

My head was aching with the stress of never ending screams
As at the age of ten years old they shattered all my dreams
With theories, methods, strategies, tactics, plans and schemes
At forty six I'm still not sure, of what this offside means.

My First Friend

There's a sense of self reflection
Or a need to find some space
A loss of ones direction
To a blank and quiet place

For a momentary second
There is silence all around
A figure in a photograph
Of an image without sound

Once blurred and somewhat hidden
Growing distant by the year
Those memories of childhood
Slowly start to reappear

From that first day at St Colum's
Nervous strangers in a class
We drank our milk together
From bottles made of glass

We sat at wooden tables
That seated five or six
Took turns on the sand pit
And played with plastic bricks

Friendships formed on Lever Road
Dave's and at the Warren
Couldn't stand the test of time
And some of us moved on

We ventured off to foreign soil
And left the Port behind
Set off on new adventures
Not knowing what we'd find

But when I met you just last year
And we stood and talked a while
I knew that we were friends for life
By your old infectious smile

It's strange what you remember
When someone you grew with dies
But that day I saw contentment
When I looked in Martins eyes

Flags. Flags And More Flags

"What's caused all the bother?"
Asked Martin from the car
"Someone's upset Peter Weir"
"This time they've gone to far"

He's running round and waving arms
And blaming Gerry Kelly
There's been a little incident
It's in the Belfast Tele

"But Peters such a pleasant bloke
You'd hardly know he's there
With his dainty little glasses
A fading tuffs of hair"

"What or who's upset him
Just you let me know
If it's one of our lot
We'll have to let them go"

No this time it's somebody else
And we're all in the clear
It happened in the early hours
So none of us were here

"Well tell me what is going on"
Said Martin getting red
With thoughts of further cutbacks
Flowing round his head

Some builders got in early
And cut a little hole
Took a tricolour from their bags
And ran it up the pole

"The flag of my dear country
Was waving in the air
That must have been a pretty sight
I wish that I was there"

Well Peters called the police in
To catch the cheeky folk
He didn't find it funny
And failed to get the joke

Ach tell that lad to wind his neck
We've bigger fish to fry
And if he's there when I arrive
I'll wipe his flaming eye

As Martin hung the mobile up
A smile came ore his face
"A flag of both sides on the roof
Would that look out of place?"

The Cliff Path

Henry O'Hara's ghostly gaze
Protects the path above the wave
No rail nor fence for which to save
The jagged rocks below

Gripped square dark brick left arm does hold
Black and brown, thick and cold
Stories whispered never told
Of jagged rocks below

The pride of Irelands northern wall
As souls of long ago do call
And cushion bones of those who fall
On jagged rocks below

Up thirty steps or more we skipped
No fear or thought should we have slipped
In foam like ice cream freshly whipped
On jagged rocks below

Respect O'Hara's weaving path
For beauty to us folk she hath
And she will spare you from her wrath
On jagged rocks below

Dancing Pants And Tackling Boots

I stand in front of mirror
As a fashion conscious teen
All pimples freshly Clearasilled
My hair lacquered and clean

The shirt I borrowed from my dad
Lies ironed and on the bed
Brilliant white with narrow stripes
In different shades of red

A lukewarm can of Tennants
On the speaker waits it turn
While I try on a jacket
Bought in Coleraine Age Concern

Hook and Bernard Sumner
Provide the backing track
As I select the dancing pants
Stay Press so snug and black

Eight hole Dr Marten's
The footwear of my roots
I dream of where the night will go
And lace my tackling boots

Tom Herron

From early morn till dark of night
You'd hear the purr of motorbike
As petrol fumes engulfed the air
I stood and whispered "we were there"

For masses came from far and near
To burger van, with crates of beer
But we had knowledge of the land
And knew the places where to stand

We crossed the burn behind Magee's
The water brushing gainst our knees
Like eager newly shaved conscripts
Then made with haste towards the pits

With sweating brow and pounding heart
The skies were loud with engine start
We clambered over stone built heap
Then sped towards the revving heat

Past the gaze of marshals eyes
We battled on towards our prize
Through leather hoards we did embark
To gain our hero's scribbled mark

No heed we paid to bright machine's
We sought the man who filled our dreams
With stickers crammed in pockets deep
In country brogue to us did speak

He took the pen in oil stained grip
And scrolled on pad immortal writ
The name to which we were all drawn
Our everlasting Tom Herron

Socialist In Marks n Spencer's

I must have had a blackout
Drifted for a while
Awoken in a frenzied sweat
In a Marks and Spencer's aisle

Quick slap my face to wake me up
Composure is the key
Pretend i know my coq au vin
And they might not notice me

Then a short sharpe jab in the upper thigh
Signals their attack
I swing around to fend them off
Preparing to strike back

I summon up the words within
To bombard the foes with fear
But thus I'm rendered powerless
When a voice says " sorry dear"

"Now pass me down that meal for one?
Sirloin steak in mustard wine
I know that combination's harsh
But I'll add a dash of thyme"

As crowds line up behind her
I feel the hand of dread
A voice cries out in anger
"Did you not hear what I said?"

"Someone call the manager
This workers downed his tools
I'll bet you he's a Corbynite
He's not following the rules"

They circle round their trollies
Chanting "zero hour contract"
Banging on their walking sticks
And "We want Tony back"

I'm searching for the exit
As their pounding at my head
With lumps of mouldy Stilton
And crusty tiger bread

Alas I fall onto the floor
And feel the cool grey tile
The last and only socialist
In a marks and spencer aisle

I Need To "Younger Up" Myself

I need to spring to action
Sharpen up my act
Get my world in motion
Bring the mojo back

Straighten out the wrinkles
Empty out the loft
Open up the windows
Shake the cobwebs off

Exercise the demons
Give my head a screw
Push against the boundaries
Shred a pound or two

Brush up on the detail
Clear the wardrobe out
Excavate the garden
Give the sea a shout

Look towards the future
Grab it by the horn
Put my house in order
Before this wain is born

Unlawfully Killed

May it come as some comfort
In the cool deep of the night
To know that the justice
For which you did fight
Was granted today
When the verdict was read
And respected the memory
Of the 96 dead

May it come as some comfort
Where the liver bird flies
To know that the tabloid
Whose scurrilous lies
Failed in its efforts
To apportion the blame
On those who had simply
Attended the game

May it come as some comfort
Now the truth is proclaimed
For the innocent sleep
As the guilty are named
While their cover-up stories
Are accepted by none
Bar the sad helpless fools
Who still purchase The Sun

May it come as some comfort
To those left behind
For in all who love football
A friend you will find
With a story to tell
Or a glass to be filled
And raised in the honour
To the unlawfully killed

She Broke My Heart On Friday Night
(so I snogged her mate on Monday)

Perhaps it was the shirt I wore
Or maybe it was fate
But she broke my heart on a Friday night
So I went and snogged her mate

It wasn't in the general plan
Or on any bucket list
But I knew alas our love was dead
So her pal I had to kiss

Not a secret peck in the locker room
Nor smooch at the local dance
Was front of all in the dinner hall
That I struck and took my chance

Well the look in her eyes I'll not forget
They were puffy crimson red
Filled with rage and then despair
As she slowly shook her head

She ran with her mate through the swinging door
Quickly followed by another
I turned and faced the jury then
And her 6ft 2 inch brother

"I'll see you Doc at half past three
Behind the chapel gate"
As he sunk his forehead in my face
And whispered "don't be late"

So a lesson here for all who care
When you feel that first heart break
If you snog her pal to get revenge
It could be a sore mistake

I Dropped My IPhone Down The Bog

My IPhone 6 went in the bog
Which wasn't very nice
I have it in the hot press
In a bag of long grain rice

I think I fried the circuits
The electrics and the sim
I've lost my rhymes and rantings
And I'm feeling rather dim

My son is now in mourning
Devastation is the word
It could have been alot worse
As I hadn't dropped a turd

All photos are deleted
Contacts flushed away
Poems I haven't printed
Won't see the light of day

So take a tip from Pablo
When your perched upon the throne
Take the papers with you
And not your mobile phone

That's Why We've No Nice Things

She turns her head as the child's IPad
Crashes on the floor
Shrieks and shouts are then exchanged
As she slams the bedroom door

Eyebrows raised and the silent wake
Is disturbed as the hall phone rings
The eldest son does then profess
"That's why we've no nice things"

Chocolate bars are scoffed in cars
Hands wiped here and there
Crisp bags stuffed behind the seats
With little thought or care

Rest assured I'll get the blame
Before the lady sings
It always seems to be my fault
That we ain't got nice things

Guzzled, half full cans of pop
Discarded where they lie
Strategically positioned
To entrap the passerby

Skinny's ripped, phones all chipped
Guitars with broken strings
Brand new trainers left outside
They just can't keep nice things

Others hold their worldly goods
In material high esteem
Clothes just thrown in a heap
Expected to be cleaned

For even festive bits and bobs
The stuff that Santa brings
Are obsolete by New Years Day
Can we please have some nice things

5.5 million

5.5 million each
That's the price of their success
Consider that when your in the queue
At the local NHS

Golden chains for immigrants
Just the ones we want to stay
If you ain't that quick off the starting blocks
You might get turned away

A positive long term investment
Is the myth the government pedals
But three hundred and fifty million pounds
For a load of bloody medals?

Shirley Crabtree, Housewives Favourite

Dickie Davis,
Lacquered hair
Big moustache
And swizzle chair
Thick blue smoke
Hangs in the air
It's Saturday's World of Sport

Four o'clock
In the afternoon
Edge of couch
Sitting room
Kent Walton
Let's out a boom
"Greetings grapple fans"

Housewives favourite
He's so hard
6 ft 6
In a leotard
As a dolly bird
Parades the card
In spandex swimming suit

Big and beefy
No six packs
Off the ropes
Then arch your backs
Let's belly slam
With Giant Haystacks

Watch Johnny Kwango's butt

Tartan blankets,
Brew in flask
Kendo
Nagasaki's mask
What's behind it,
Don't dare ask
There's a tattoo on his brow

Widows peak
And tight black pants
McManus has them
In a trance
Head locked round the ring
He'll prance
Mum's shouting at the box

Oh, it's all part
Of my history
Teleprinter
Then your tea
Cod and chips
Upon your knee
Housewives favourite, Big Daddy

One Day

One day I'll not worry about money
One day the butter will be in the fridge
One day there will be no bills
One day tea bags will be plentiful
One day he'll run to me, not the IPad
One day the phone will not ring
One day I'll score and they will cheer
One day clothes will be irrelevant
One day all will be remote
One day the car will start
One day the phone will ring
One day they will make their beds
One day it will fit
One day I'll understand
One day the first word I say will be yes
One day he'll bring socks down
On that one day, I'll know enough

Supermarket Love Affair

She waited in line for a scratch card
Slowly twisting her hand through her hair
I munched on a smoked bacon sandwich
Transfixed by her welcoming stare

Her sausage on brown toasted wheat grain
Did little to dampen the mood
As she wiped a small crumb from her sweet lips
I worshiped the ground where she stood

Past newspaper stands we did wander
Heading straight towards carrots and peas
When she whispered I love you my darling
I nearly went weak at the knees

Well she prodded and squeezed at the oranges
The onions, tomatoes and pears
Hit me a slap on the backside
Ignoring the gasps and the stares

I smiled and adjusted my glasses
Lifted a pre packed courgette
Headed towards frozen produce
With an extra wee spring in my step

By the pet food she caused a commotion
When she gave me a peck on the cheek
A girl on the check out did beckon
The manager from the boutique

He chased us from tinned fruit to biscuits
Caught up with us by the eclairs
Brought over a small man called Derek
From his stand at the top of the stairs

Together they issued instruction
To leave his food store at great haste
For our savoury shows of affection
Had left in his mouth a sour taste

I grabbed this fine lass by the Pringles
And gave her the kiss of my life
Proclaiming to all who had gathered
Wise up folks, this is my wife!

Just A Love Poem

I Love your eyes
I love your lips
I love the way you
Shake your hips
I love the way
You wear your jeans
I love the fact
You fill my dreams
I love it when you
Say good night
I love just how
You make life right
Every freckle on your face
The way you move things
Out of place
I love your brand new
Denim skirt
I love you so
My heart does hurt

54 Days

Our lives were thrown
Into a chaotic cycle of fear
As on the hallway tile
A six by nine inch envelope
Did routinely appear
Was not emblazoned with "CAUTION"
Open tentatively with care
It was in between some co-op mail,
Just sort of lying there

Calls were made to relatives
Some we hadn't seen for years
One way conversations
Interspersed with bouts of tears
Reassuring loved ones
Who offered their support
"Let's not think of worse case scenarios
Till we get the full report"

Appointments hastily arranged
As our lives paused in silent dread
I cannot accurately describe the pictures
Flashing through my head
Images of growing old together
Floating out of reach
A single set of footprints
Stretching out across an isolated beach

Quiet words of comfort
From NHS Angels passing by
My hopeless inability
To ease her need to constantly cry
We sat not really knowing
How this movie picture plays
How much we grown closer
In these fifty four long days

Boxes ticked, dates fixed
Prayers said with genuine dedication
This was no five team
Last one accumulator prediction
This was real grown up pain
And edge of seat
Staring in the eyes
Of possible everlasting defeat

City hospital, day fifty four
Fifteen minutes until eleven
I raised the last "please God just one more"
Up to heaven
She grips my hand
He smiles and speaks the sweetest words
I've yet to hear
" Your all clear"

ABOUT THE AUTHOR

Pablo Doherty grew up in the north coast seaside town of Portstewart in County Derry before leaving for Belfast in 1987. Pablo moved to Liverpool, England in the late 80's before returning to Belfast in 1996. Crimes Against Poetry is his third collection of poems from the Shouting At The Sea series, following on from "Shells" and "They Use To Paint The Kerb Stones".

Pablo is married with five chidren and lives in County Armagh

Printed in Poland
by Amazon Fulfillment
Poland Sp. z o.o., Wrocław

58938574R00078